TAKE YOUR TIME

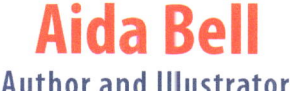

Aida Bell
Author and Illustrator

AuthorHouse™
1663 Liberty Drive
Bloomington, IN 47403
www.authorhouse.com
Phone: 1 (800) 839-8640

Published by AuthorHouse 10/07/2016

ISBN: 978-1-5246-4341-6 (sc)
ISBN: 978-1-5246-4342-3 (e)

Print information available on the last page.

Any people depicted in stock imagery provided by Thinkstock are models,
and such images are being used for illustrative purposes only.
Certain stock imagery © Thinkstock.

This book is printed on acid-free paper.

Because of the dynamic nature of the Internet, any web addresses or links contained in this book may have changed
since publication and may no longer be valid. The views expressed in this work are solely those of the author and do not
necessarily reflect the views of the publisher, and the publisher hereby disclaims any responsibility for them.

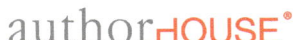

Dedication page

This book is dedicated to my grandfather. His aspiration for the American dream was never fulfilled in his lifetime. I hope he is looking down on me with a big happy smile!

Nothing is instant
Great things take time to happen
Just look at nature all around us

A day is gradual, with a light and night rhythm
It starts with a welcoming sunrise
Then comes a bright noon Sun
Slowly moves towards a soothing sunset
To finally end in a starry night

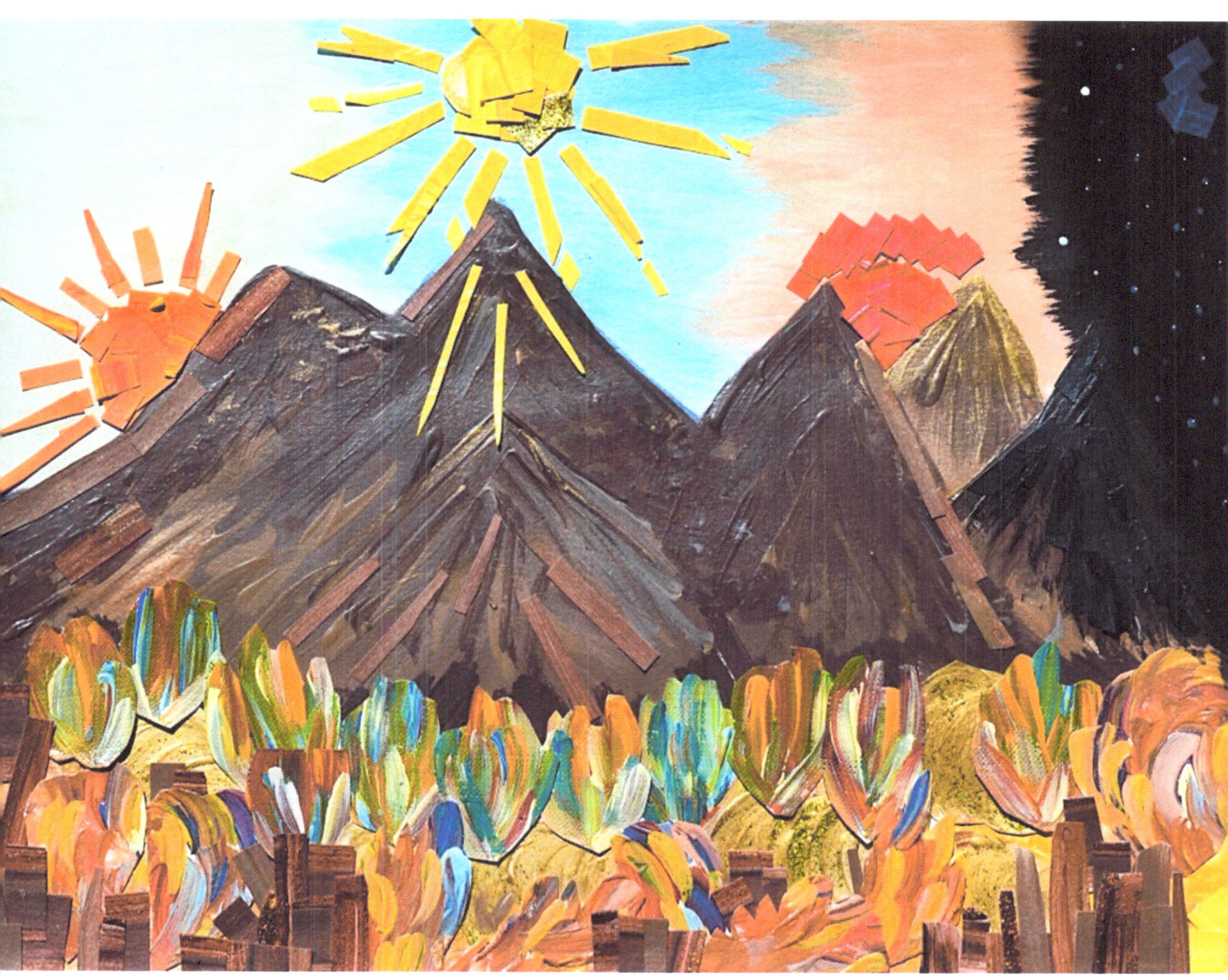

A year is a seasonal dance performed by
A mellow, golden autumn
A magical, white winter
A musical spring with its colorful opening act
And a fun, warm summer

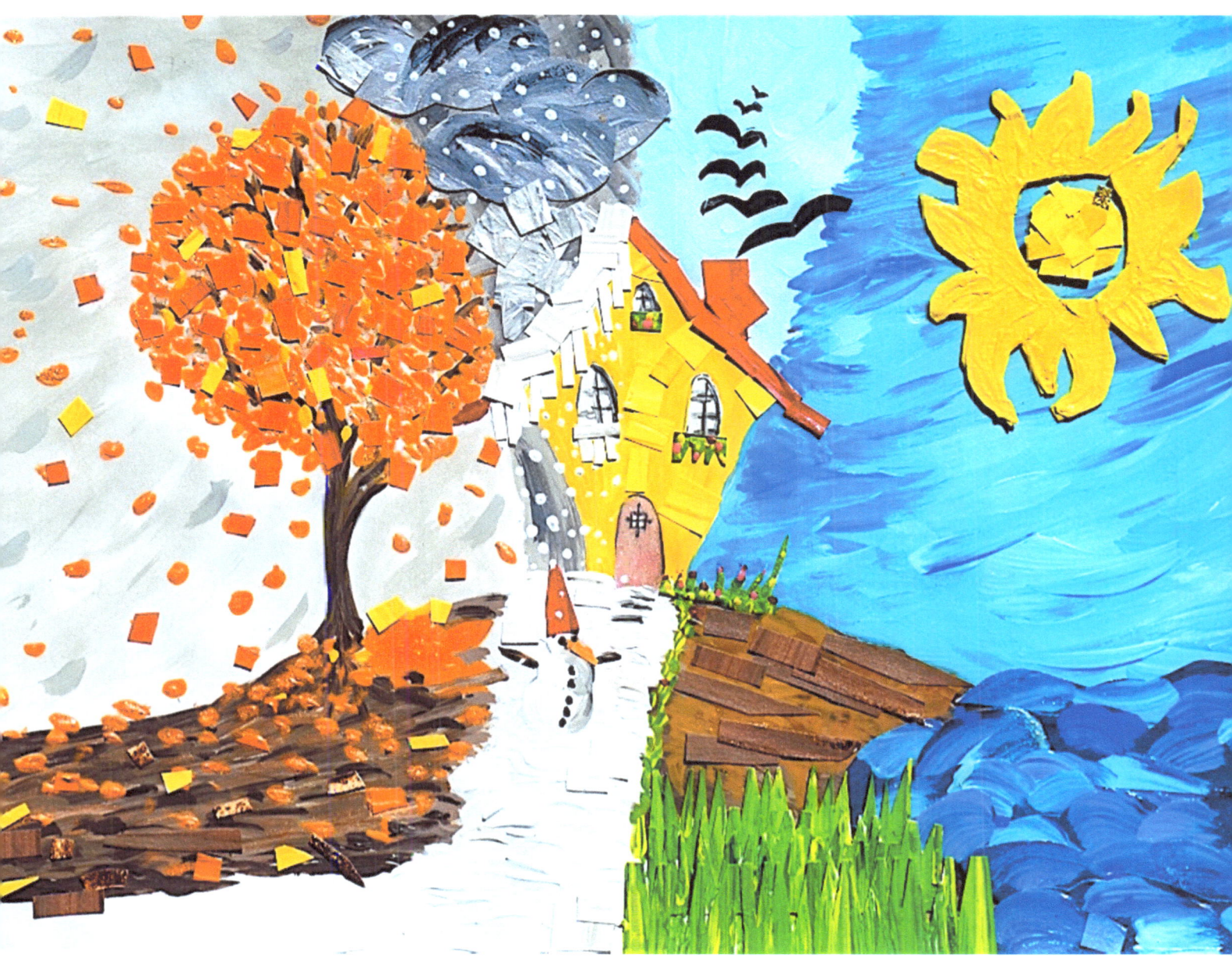

Growing crops takes hard work
First, turn over the soil and plant seeds everywhere
Fertilize carefully and water lovingly
Have faith in Mother Nature
Wait patiently for the seeds to thrive
To finally, harvest gratefully

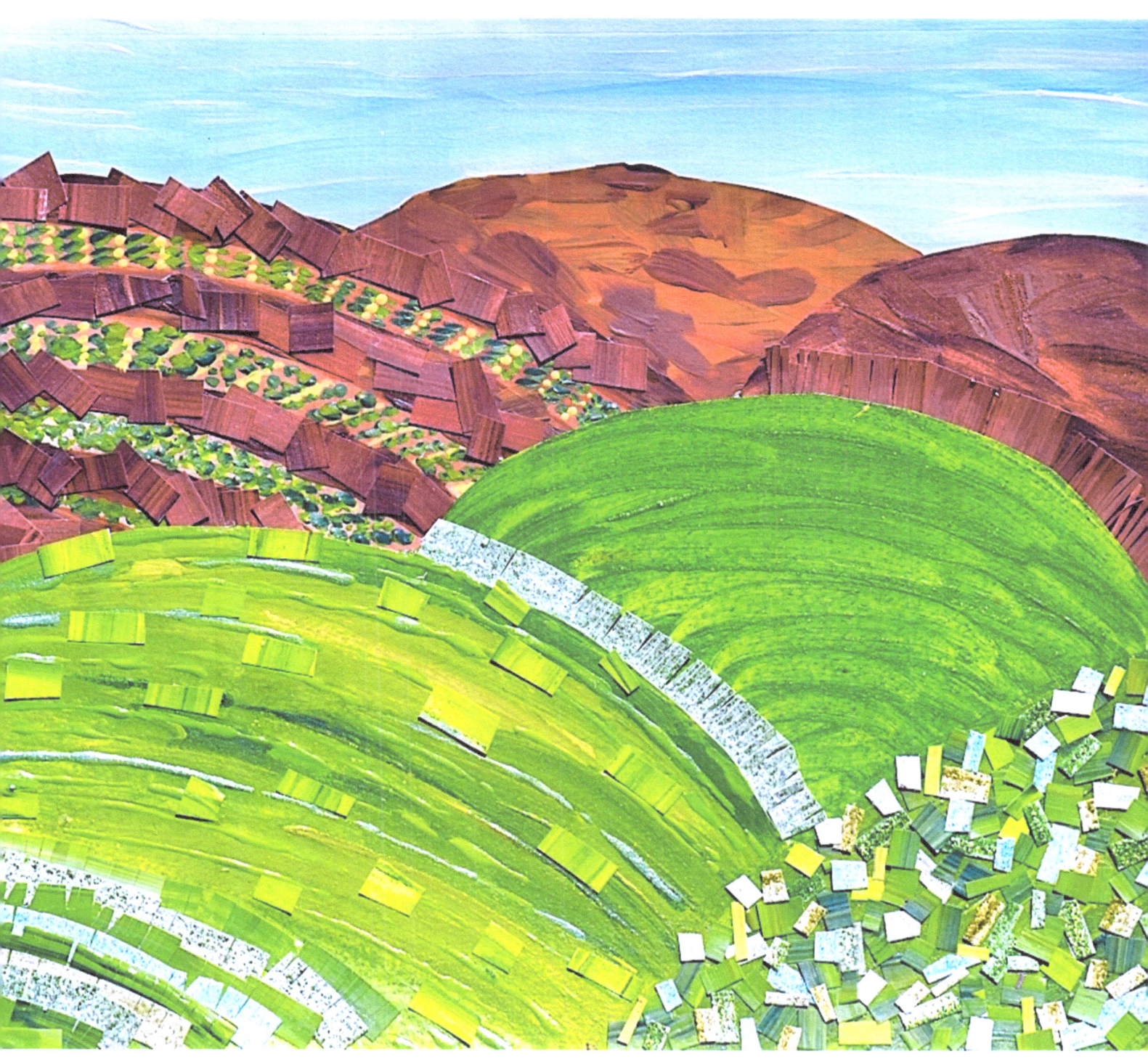

Planets dance around the Sun at their own pace
It takes a year for Earth to complete a full orbit
About a month for the Moon to circle Earth
A day for Earth to rotate around itself
Imagine! Hundreds of years for Neptune to revolve around the sun

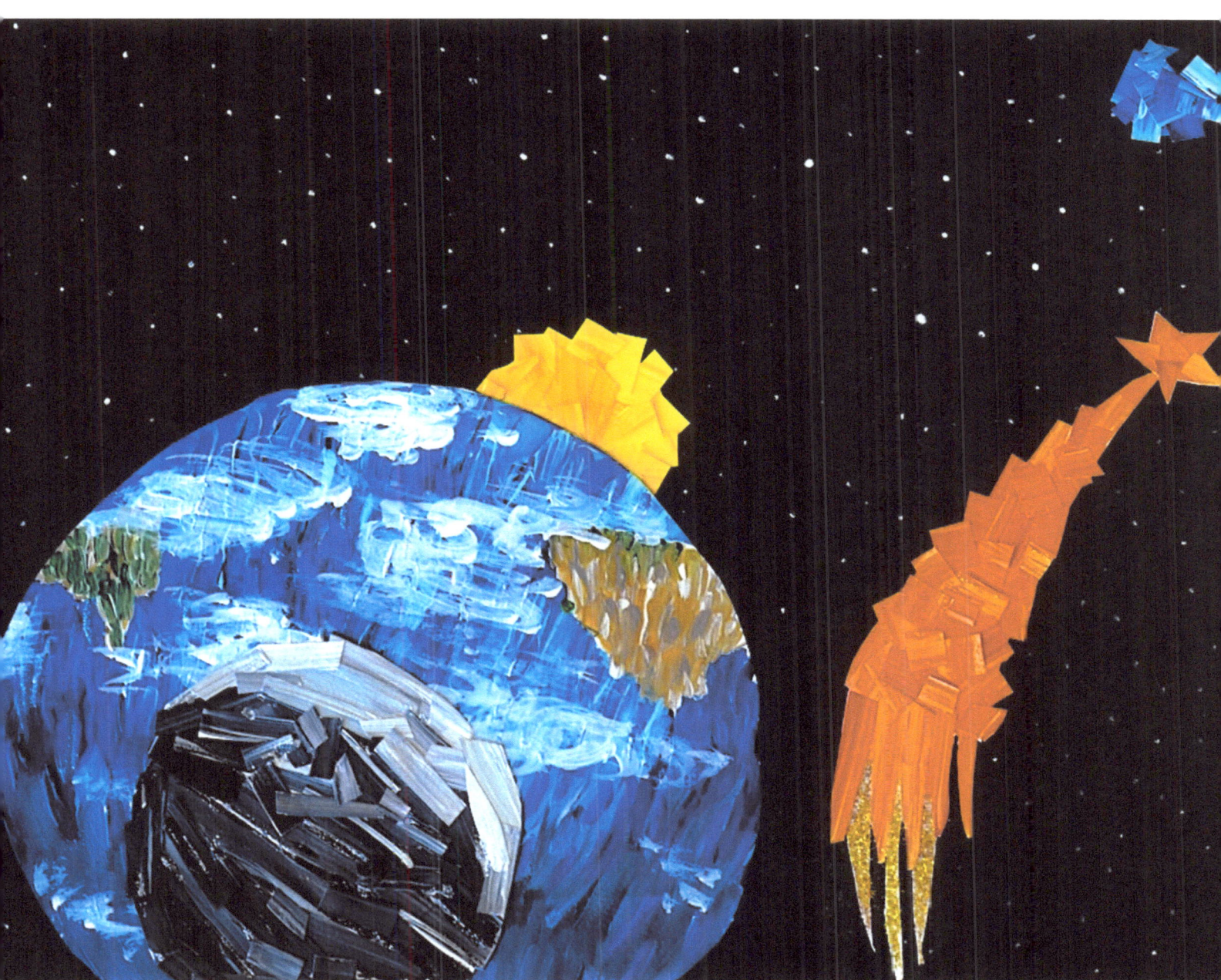

A butterfly transforms in its own terms
Each egg, laid on a leaf, becomes a caterpillar
It makes its own cocoon where it hides for days to weeks.
Only when the time is right,
It emerges into a graceful butterfly

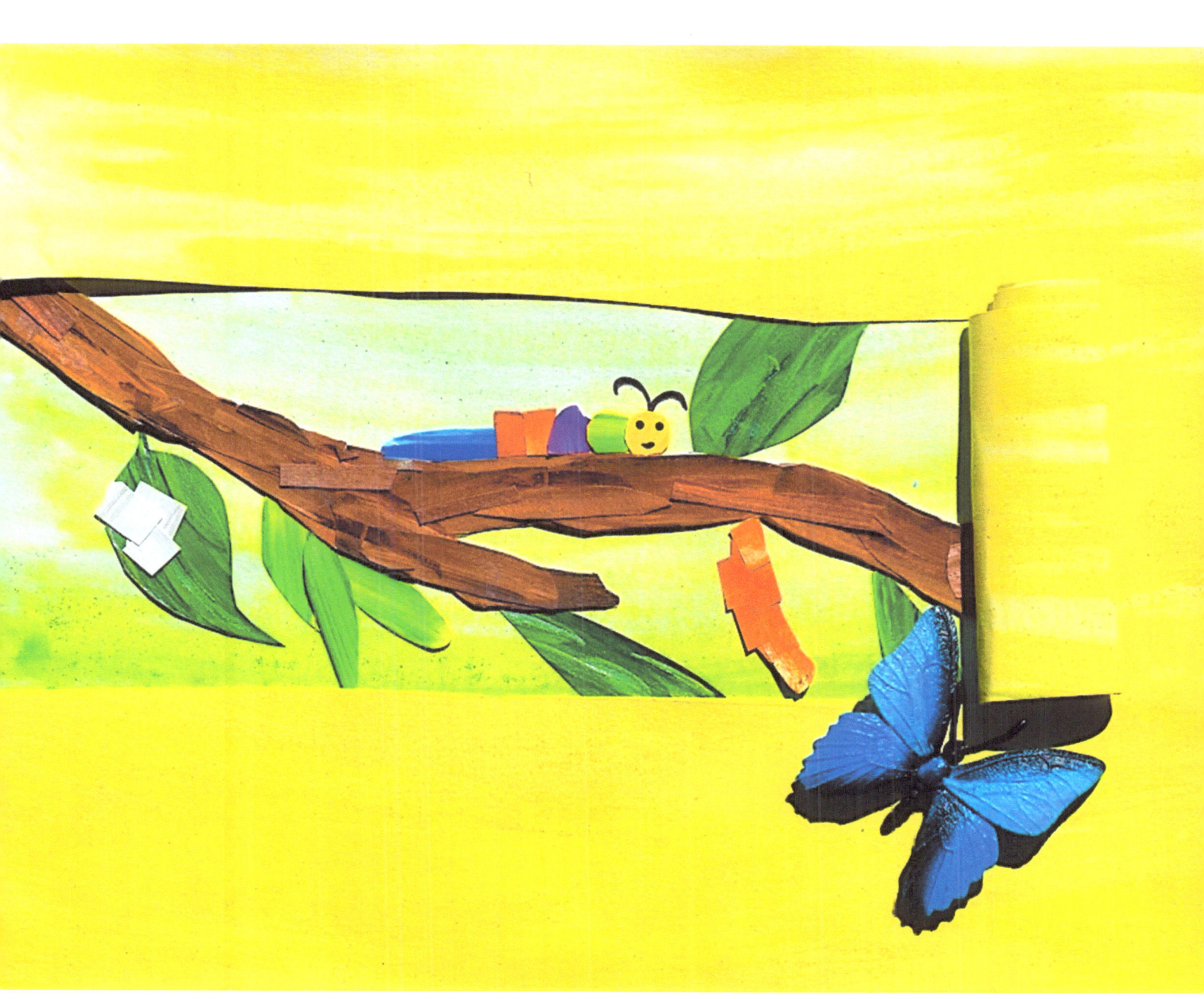

It takes time to learn
Preschool - with its ABCs
Elementary - more than 123
Middle school - learning how to grow
High school - finding what you love
College - pursuing more, much more
I guess learning never stops.

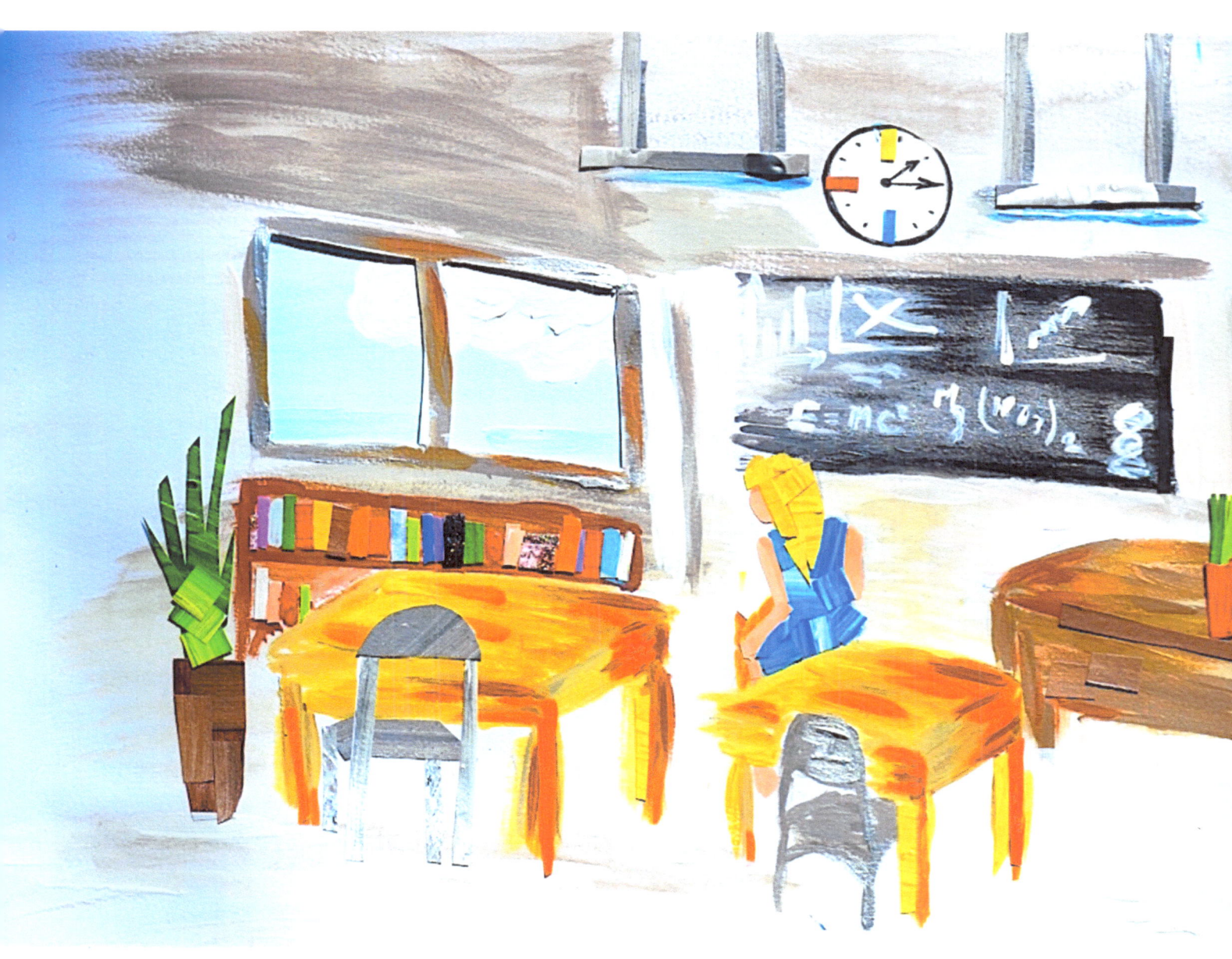

Rushing does not mean you are moving forward
So remember to always take your time,
Enjoy the dance, the rhythms, the growth.

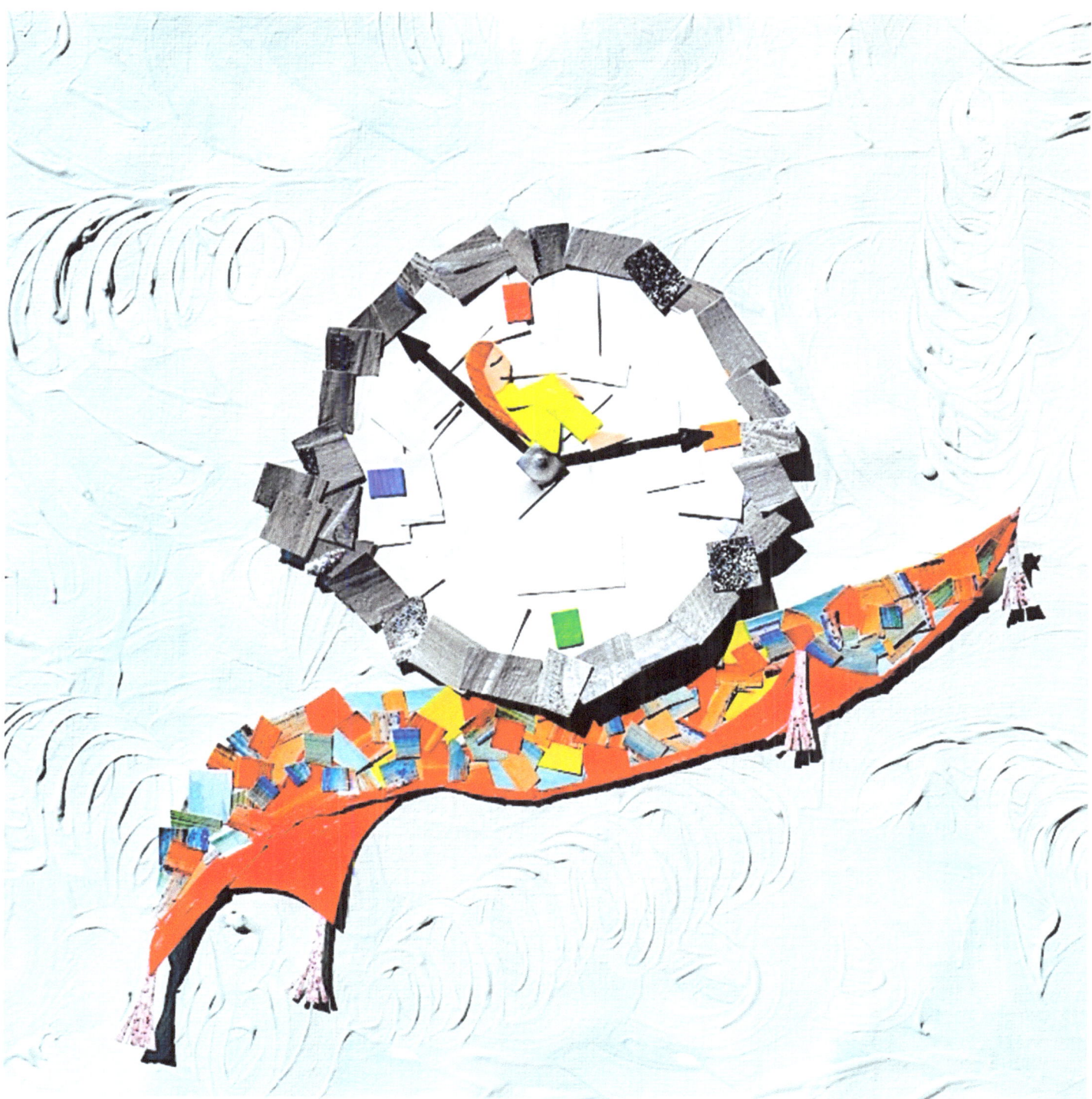

Can you answer these questions?

What is your favorite season and why?

Does the Moon turn around itself like Earth?

What is your favorite subject in school?

Do you have a hobby, a passion?

If you close your eyes and imagine, how do you picture time?

Let me know your answers on my FB page
Aida Bell Author/Artist.

www.ingramcontent.com/pod-product-compliance
Lightning Source LLC
Chambersburg PA
CBHW050437180526
45159CB00006B/2568